My Foundation
Second Edition

Melanie "Babydoll" Wallace

TABLE OF CONTENTS

My Foundation

My foundation is about where you come from and how to get to the next level. Ways to make a plan and how to follow through. My foundation is the motivation you need to start where you are and to get to where you want to be.

In this life, this journey, you need to be open to things, and you need to be able to handle all situations. This comes from experience and just living and learning. You need to be able to handle yourself, know what and how to speak. How do you do this? Talk to a lot of diverse people, at school, church, wherever. You need to be comfortable around anyone and everyone and able to carry on a conversation.

In this book, you will get a road map to success and suggestions to refine your current skills and talents.

First off, I am by no means telling you I have all the answers. I just know that I am at a place in my life where I am truly happy. I also know that this journey for me is still moving.

I was raised in Toledo, Ohio. My parents are the hardest-working people you will ever know. "You have to get your education to make it in this world," they always told me. My father worked at a factory, my mom worked as a librarian/secretary for the school district, and she played the piano for her church. They owned rental properties, and my dad did all the repairs on the properties and dealt with the tenants. Every weekend, I recall going to the properties with my parents to do the yard work. Even as early as six, I remember running around to help by getting extra bags, getting tools or whatever I was told. I was the youngest of 4. The oldest is a strong sista who does things by the book. Did everything the way that my parents wanted. She is currently a retired teacher. The 2nd oldest, she tends to be a loner and is also a retired teacher. Then my brother, a cool dude to hang with, works with the youth. Then me, well, I'm kind of an overachiever.

Before I get into me, there is one other thing that was a regular source in our home, that was God. We were brought up in the church, and for most people brought up in the church, you know, that is something that always stays with you. I remember joining the church at 6 with my brother and getting into the choir. My mother played the piano, and my sister played the organ. We were at church more than we were home, it seems, and I loved it. I remember being at the house when my mom had rehearsals. I loved music, and I loved voices. I remember one Sunday, no one wanted to lead a song. My mom was mad, so she had me lead something. I had been begging her for years, but I think she thought I was too young and just kind of blew me off. But this particular Sunday, no one wanted to sing, and she was desperate. She gave me the words, and I belted out all that I could. Everyone, including me, was shocked at what came out. See, I had been singing in the shower, or in the inside porch we had, but never to an audience. I thought I was good, but it wasn't until that day that we all realized that I had something.

After that day, I began to sing solos, and I started to look for any reason to sing in public. I would sing in church, festivals, plays at school, anywhere I could get exposure. The bottom line was that I felt I had done everything in this area, and it was time to try something else. I like to take risks, and I like to have the experience. As of 2013, I am now an International Entertainer, living abroad. In addition to music, I tutor (English, Math & IELTS). I believe I am who I am because of my upbringing, but I don't use that as an excuse to further myself in anything. I am an adult now, and I decided many years ago that I was going to change my life and live it to the fullest by following my dreams. In 2001, I was working as a manager at Zales Corp (The Diamond Store). I was on my way to becoming a District Manager and eventually a Regional Manager. The money was excellent; I had finished all of my goals of getting a Bachelor's Degree, having a Managing Cosmetology License, and had gained so much business experience. The only thing that had not been accomplished yet was that I had never lived anywhere else except Toledo, and I wanted to see where the music could take me.

I was singing every chance I had, but I was not focusing on it or nourishing my career. I got a call out of the blue to tour in Japan. I decided that was the change I needed. I was happy where I was, but felt that I needed more world experience to better prepare myself for whatever was to come. I wound up leaving everything I knew to see if I could cut it in the "Real World". The Japan experience (2001), actually woke me up, and that is what led me on the current journey that I am on. "We only have one life to live, and I am going to live the hell out of it."

Now that I had all the skills, the balls, and God on my side, after going to Japan 3 times, I decided to change the scenery and embarked on a move to Los Angeles. I knew one person there who claimed they could help me; as time would tell, he couldn't even help himself. But I never expected him or anyone to help me anyway, so that way I never get let down.

He did, however, set up my living arrangements when I first arrived. Thank God for that; it made it easier for me to focus on getting set up in L.A. After about a month and a half, I finally moved into my own apartment and sent for my car and personal belongings.

I had a plan, set goals, and never once looked back. I had faith, undeniable faith.

Whether or not you believe in God is your choice, but believe in yourself always.

Love yourself

Haven't we all heard the saying, "Love yourself first, and then others will follow"? Believe it, this is a true statement. If you are secure with yourself, you will attract individuals who share the same theme. The first thing you need to do is love yourself unconditionally. Whether you're overweight, too skinny, not smart, or shy. Love yourself first. You have what you have, work with it. If you don't think you're smart, get more education, read more books, and challenge yourself. Some things you can change, some you can't. Figure out which is which. Life will get easier the sooner you figure that out. What you can't change, learn to deal with it, make it work for you. The goal is to find the best you and bring it out.

This is not going to happen overnight; it's a journey, you need to realize that and continue to work on yourself. The reality is that the way you are raised has a lot to do with how you are.

I learned a lot of things over the years, and I'm still pressing forward. I believe that you need to look into your soul and figure out who you are. I am who I am because I decided to make my own rules. At first, I had resistance from my family. They eventually got on board when they realized that they could not control me and that I was going to do it my way. Funny thing: a lot of the things my parents said, based on experience, were correct. But I didn't always listen to my parents' suggestions, but the funny thing is, I listen to them now. My mom always pushed me to attend college. If I didn't have my Degree, I don't think I could have made it this far. Of course, knowing me, I would have found a way. Having a backup saved me many days.

Figure out

Figure out what you want to do and have a backup. Knowing at a young age, I played with my dolls every day. I would do their hair, teach them a lesson daily, and then sing to them later on. I have worked in and run a successful beauty salon. I work as a Substitute Teacher and mentor to children and young adults. I travel internationally, entertaining and bringing happiness to all types of people. It wasn't always that way.

I have worked all types of jobs, gaining all types of experiences. Some of the positions I have worked are: Administrative Assistant, Accountant, Bank Teller, Casino Worker, Receptionist, Telemarketer, Janitor, Retail Sales Associate, Warehouse Worker, Factory Worker, Training Manager and Assistant Manager, Asst. to DM, and many other titles. No matter what position I was in, I gave 150%. In most jobs, the manager noticed me, and I was the one who would motivate people. "Make it happen" has been my slogan as long as I can remember. I just see it this way, anything is possible, you just have to find a way to make it happen. Everything in my life has been a challenge to accomplish, but I have never given up, and I have always kept my focus on the prize. Don't get me wrong, I have my days when I just want to give up and "go home". Then I reflect on all of my accomplishments and think, "How the (bleep) did I get this far?" Only by faith, believing in God and myself. Setting goals, making a plan, and sticking to it. Often, I have to look at my plan and rework it. Hey, things don't always go the way you want, trust me. Of course, that's the great thing about this life; you need to be prepared for anything. Take the ride and see where you go. Have a plan, have a backup plan, have an emergency plan in place. Never give up and never look back, unless you need to remind yourself where you came from.

Writing a Journal

I guess in my family, I'm considered the black sheep of the family. I'm not that bad, but I tend to go out on a limb. I find myself going for what I want, rather than what everyone else wants for me. I tried it their way, I found success, but I wasn't totally happy. I went to college, I got a great job, and I found that I wasn't totally fulfilled. That's when I stopped myself and started writing a journal.

Sometimes this is a great method to see where you are in life and find out what things you are repeating. A great tool to get a handle on your life, to get yourself focused on one main thing you need to accomplish. Years ago, I wrote down what I wanted in life. I made a blueprint of how I could accomplish it. As the years go on, I reflect on where I was by reading what I was thinking years ago. I regroup and update anything that I have done, and start to work on the next thing.

As time goes on, I have added and removed items from the list of things I have accomplished. I am proud of where I am today, but I am just beginning. My journey is really just starting. I have tons of stories, pictures, and memories to share. I have no problem sharing, in hopes that someone can get something out of it. Get to know yourself; the sooner in life you can realize who you are, the better. You are special, you have something to offer. You may not know what yet, but with life experiences and being open to trying new things, you will figure it out. Maybe you have wise adults around you who may help you realize your dreams. Sometimes, close individuals around you can spot your talents.

Notes

Following your dreams

Don't get me wrong, things aren't always going to go your way. You need to accept that, maybe God has something else for you. What you can do is continue to focus on the prize, pray, or meditate. See yourself in the situation. See it already happening. Focus on the positive, focus on your gift. For example, your talent or gift may be helping people. You need to figure out in what capacity. Well, make a list of ways to help people. Helping at a rest home, helping with children, and helping at church.

You may also be an excellent cook. Combine the 2 talents where you help them by feeding them. Churches always need and want people to help with events. You may start your own catering business, eventually. The thing is, find a place for you. This may take months or years, but the goal is to be truly happy doing what you enjoy. If you can't find a situation for you, make it up.

Make it up as you go

I didn't have all the answers when I started. As I am going on this journey, I find that I am figuring it out as I go. I'm making up my own way; there is no right or wrong way. Just get out there and make it happen. For me, I knew I wanted to sing and travel (First main goal). I did everything I could in Ohio, Michigan, Indiana, and New York. As far as performing went, in fact, a lot of performances were for free. I let everyone know that I wanted to travel. Eventually, I landed my first tour to Japan, Tokyo (2001). This led to 4 total tours to Japan. I made tons of connections, which helped me later to move to Los Angeles and then Las Vegas. No matter where I am, I promote myself. I tell people what I do and where I want to go. Always, somebody knows someone who knows someone who may be able to help me. I have a theory that I must follow all leads. They may not be able to help me, but they may be able to send me to somebody who can.

My focus is to meet as many people as possible; I believe it's in the numbers. The more people you meet, the better chance that someone will lead you to the right situation. In the meantime, I continue to put myself out there. I answer ads in the paper, online, or on bulletin boards at music halls or studios. I go out to clubs, open mics, musical events, and anything where I can meet people. I feel that the right situation will present itself, so I just continue to pray and focus on the next opportunity. Sometimes, I have to pass on tours, because the money's not right or I am finishing something. You make the rules, so don't just take anything; make sure it will keep you on the road to your goals.

Trust me, you know if it's right for you. Always cover yourself, whatever you do. Make sure you have extra money or an empty credit card, because it would be a shame to be caught overseas with no money. Luckily for me, I always get off the plane with at least 10 agents to connect with once I get into a country. I have never had an issue this far, but I always say be prepared. Take a chance, be prepared. Cover yourself at all costs. Then you can enjoy yourself and have the experience of a lifetime. Live your life and follow your dreams.

Notes

Knowing Yourself

You need to look at yourself in the mirror and be honest with yourself. Ask yourself these questions: What do you want out of life? What are your dreams? Where do you see yourself in 5 years or 10 years?

What do you need to do to get to your goals? These are just good questions to start with. You need to get your life started towards your goals. So we might as well start somewhere. Don't think about what you have done; it's what you will do. You have the power to do whatever you want; you just need to be clear on what you want first. Then you can make up the plans to get there. Look at today as being the start, let's go. It's never too late to start. No more excuses. Figure out what you want to do and make a plan to get there. Some people try to use excuses such as, "They weren't raised to accomplish anything in life." You are what you are, face it. You have the chance to come out of the ashes. Don't use anyone or anything as an excuse for you. For years, my parents said that if I left the city of Toledo, they wouldn't support me. For years, my sisters, brother, and I was scared to venture out anywhere, believing that we wouldn't have any support. I still remember leaving for Los Angeles, scared to death. But I felt I had to do it to get to the experiences that I needed to advance my career. It worked, and surprisingly, my parents have helped me financially and emotionally. I thank God for that. I still don't know how I would have gotten this far without their help. Actually, many people on my journey have come forward and helped. I have been given a laptop, money, dinners, great connections, and lots of emotional support. I have to say, when people see you doing something, they will try to help you if they can. I am truly blessed; a lot of people believe in me and see that I will "make it." What they don't understand is that I have already made it. I am still moving on, and the future is getting brighter. I don't measure my success by money; I measure it by my happiness. I am truly happy, and I can't wait to see what happens next. It's all about letting go and seeing what will be. A lot of times, I did shows for free. I did things for free to get exposure and to meet people. As time has passed, I still do appearances for free, but I focus on paid events. I am at the point where I feel it is time to build my resume with great experiences.

Finding Yourself

You need to know yourself. Be honest with yourself and be real. Make a list of what you like. Make a list of your talents and your skills. Then figure out a way to do it. You may have to work a "real job" as you are setting up your dream job. But eventually, you can turn your dream job into a reality. But remember, it may not take a week, a month, or even a year. You have to stick with it no matter what. I was told many times do what you love, and the money will come. I believe that, and slowly but surely, it has been like that.

Once you make your list, you should talk to at least 10 people around you. Ask them what they think your skills and talents are. What they think you would be good at. I remember at college going to the counselor and taking a job placement test. Basically, it pinpoints what your strengths are and what you would be good at. Between the test and the opinions of close family and friends, you should be able to figure out what your focus should be. The final decision is yours, but you do need to listen to the comments of others. Sometimes other people can see what your strengths are.

There is also one other thing that should influence your decision about what you will do in life. Your passion!

Your Passion

What do you have a passion for? What do you like to do? What do you dream of? You need to find your passion! You need to figure out what you can't live without. Be honest with yourself, and you will find your true passion! What is your passion, the thing you love to do no matter what? Your passion is something you would do for free. It doesn't even seem like work because you enjoy it so much. You need to dig deep and discover your passion. You probably already know what it is, now it is time to focus on the next step. Making your passion into a dream job is the next step that takes time. You will have to be patient and work hard to get to the next step. So just hang in there and stay focused. Just think, knowing is half the battle. You need to focus on your passion and try to figure out where to go next. Set up a plan and focus on it. Once you decide what your passion is, it's time to get out there and gain exposure.

Do research on your passion on the internet and by talking to others who are in your field. I always talk to other people who are in my field.

Whether they have been doing it for 30 plus years or for two years. Everyone can give their knowledge from their experiences, and you can always learn something from everyone. I thank God for all the people I have met and all the stories that were shared. Believe me, those stories help to make you a stronger person. If you ever come into a situation like the stories you heard, you can deal with it. Sometimes stories prepare us for the future. I also like to hear other people's opinions on things. I try to see things in a different light. I try to be open and not judge. I will give anybody a chance to express themselves and give their opinion. I don't have to agree, but I will respect your opinion. I think being open enough to listen to people and still having your own opinions is the way to go. In this life, this journey, you need to be open to things, and you need to be able to handle all situations. This comes from experience and just living and learning. You need to be able to handle yourself, know what and how to speak.

How do you do this? Talk to a lot of diverse people, at school, church, wherever. You need to be comfortable around anyone and everyone and able to carry on a conversation.

Learning new tricks

What I am finding out by living overseas is that people don't stay around. Most of the people I meet stay for a while and leave. When I meet someone new, and they ask how long I plan to be here, I say 6 to 8 years. They look at me like I'm crazy. Why?? The reason is that I have goals to accomplish, and I think it will take that long. To be honest, I'm not completely sure. But bottom line, I'm not leaving until I have all the things I want. So it could be longer. I have goals and things are really happening for me overseas, so this is where I will call home for a while. By me, making a commitment to stay here and be a part of the community, I have noticed I am getting a lot of free education. I work at a tutoring place, and they have offered free training. I love free things, especially something that is of value and can be used in the US. So I am certified to teach Robotics to kids. Robotics is huge in the States, and it's a great way to introduce your kids to programming a robot. This is where the future is going, and I want to be there.

Believe me, I was not looking into teaching Robotics, but it fell into my lap. This is an important lesson: if someone offers you free classes, take them. Worst thing, you don't like it, but you have a new skill. It's important to learn everything you can; you never know when it will come in handy.

Building on your talents

I believe that the more you know, the better prepared you will be. I love to sing, and I continue to push my voice. I also dance and can tell a joke or two. Now that I feel that I have developed my voice, even though I am still perfecting it, I am now working on learning to play the piano. I would like to accompany myself. This will help me not to have to depend on someone and will make me more valuable. I did try when I was younger, but didn't understand the value of being a one-woman show. But now I'm ready to try it; this time I feel that I'm much more serious and determined. So we will see what happens. The point is to work with what you've got. So if you can't sing, then please don't. But maybe you have talents elsewhere. You need to do an inventory of what you can do. It seems silly, but somebody doesn't know what they have and sometimes needs someone else to point it out. For example, I was at my favorite restaurant, and a very cute waiter came over to ask for our order. When he opened his mouth, my girlfriend and I just melted. He actually sounded like Barry White, no joke. We immediately asked if he sings or does commercials. He said he had just moved overseas and was struggling to get work. We told him how his voice made us feel and that he should be trying to do radio, voice-overs, or something. He said that he always gets that, so we asked whether he was going to pursue it. The first thing he said was, "I don't have any money, but I would like to try." Well, as I told him, the first thing is he has a desire, that's the first thing. As far as money, if you are low on cash, figure out a way to get what you want in exchange for another service. For instance, I needed to record tracks for my demo, but could not afford the total amount to get the album done. So I struck up a relationship with a local DJ. In exchange for tracks, I sang on the DJ's tracks. This is how I got my first couple of demos. Also, it's advertising for me. Now I have my voice on the DJ's tracks, and when he played them at parties, I would get work from rappers who needed hooks.

So this was another one of my side hustles. Using what you have to get exposure.

Notes

Be honest with yourself

This was a very hard one for me. I was raised with great parents and grandparents, and they basically told me what to do. Of course, in hindsight, they were absolutely right, well, about one thing. All my parents knew was to work hard, and you will succeed. Get an education and have a skill, and you will never have to worry. They were absolutely right about that. But they never told me to find something you loved, your passion. It was teaching because it's steady and there will always be work. They were right on that, so going into the education field was smart. But by not listening to them and exploring on my own, I found my passion, which is music. I have been able to create a very exciting and lucrative business out of music. My dream was just to do music for a living, which for me has been so unstable to do only music. I find that having both teaching and singing has been surprisingly enjoyable. I don't have to stress about money because the teaching thing is pretty steady.

Actually, funny thing, since I left the U.S. and decided to live abroad, the music has been very steady too. So I'm blessed because I had a backup plan and I had the drive to make it happen.

What do you want out of life?

About 25 years ago, I sat down and wrote out what I wanted to do. For me, I have to see it in writing to make myself accountable. I thought I would only be doing music, but as the years went by, I added new things that worked and deleted things that didn't work. Now that the teaching is added, I decided to take more classes. Learn more, try more, bottom line, be the best in my field, is what I strive for. I feel good about helping students, and I learn too. I also started asking myself, " How do I feel?" This is a very important question to me. Because if I feel good about something, I pursue it. If not, I drop it and move on. I found out that I thrive when I feel good about myself. When I don't, I only bring on stress and anxiety. I want to be happy!!! I have a very happy spirit, and I am very optimistic. Thankfully, I had that mindset because I could not see it in the beginning. For years, I told anyone that would listen, I would be singing overseas and traveling the world. Most just laughed at me, and others would ask, "How"? For a long time, I was waiting for someone to help me. But that never really happened, but once people saw that I was actually doing things to put myself in a position to go. Then I got help. You can't expect someone to help you if you aren't doing something to help yourself. I was very active in the community, going out to open mics, auditions, anything, anywhere to get exposure. I was, and I am great at following a lead, networking, and staying in touch with people. I am also easy to get along with, and I'm always making someone laugh. That has helped me in this journey, trust me.

If you fail, keep pushing on!

I have failed. Most things I tried at first, I failed. But I just keep going back and figuring it out.

Just like riding a bike, you will not get it the first time. It takes practice. I'm still learning, and I love learning new things. I feel you need to always be trying new things. How can you tell if it's for you if you don't try? The key is to never give up, even when you are down. It seems to me that, as soon as I'm about to even think about quitting, I get a breakthrough. Or some kind of sign to hang on.

Be happy no matter what

The sooner you realize this, the better. Be happy no matter what; it could be worse. Don't get me wrong, things aren't always going to go your way. You need to accept that, in fact, maybe God has something else for you. Look around you today, no matter what city, state, or country, it's not hard to find unhappy people. The goal is not to be one of them. I am generally a happy person, and so is my mom. She used to always say "Doesn't take much to make me happy." I find this is true for me, too. I enjoy doing things alone or with a partner. It's nice to have someone to do things with, but I'm ok if it's just me. It doesn't bother me now. But when I was in my 20's, I hated going out alone, I just wouldn't go. But after missing out on concerts, parties, and things I wanted to do. I just decided that I didn't want to miss things anymore. This really helped me to be able to move to another country. I was not afraid, it was a great adventure. Also, it helps I make friends easily, and I find like minded people.

Notes

____

____

____

____

____

____

____

____

____

____

____

____

____

____

____

____

____

____

____

What worked for me was when I began substitute teaching, which made me comfortable around different people and situations. Now it is just second nature.

Asking for help

No one knows all the answers, but an individual who can ask questions learns a lot. I ask questions all the time. I am always trying to learn something new. I enjoy meeting people and learning their story. I think it is very interesting to see how we have made it to this point. I have learned that when you ask questions, people see you in a different light. For me, people would see that I was trying to improve, not only to help me reach my goal but also to take a special interest in my progress. I find that everyone has a dream. But most feel they don't have the time to pursue it or won't invest in themselves. Sometimes it's not about money; it can be time used. You have to spend either time or money, and sometimes both, to invest in your dreams. Think of it this way, if it's something you want, you'll enjoy it so much that time will fly. The bottom line is to make yourself happy and do what you dream of.

Being alone, not lonely

I believe that there is someone out there for everyone. But I don't believe in settling. I find that when I focus on myself, and I'm happy, I attract a better quality of man. I also find that when you settle for less than you want, you tend to bring drama into your life because you are never going to be satisfied with the outcome. So you are better off clearing your mind and your life of the things you don't want. This allows room for the things or people you want in your life. The best thing is to work on yourself, and you will attract the kind of person or people you want in your life. When you are truly living your life and working on yourself, others who are doing the same will come into your life. At the same time, when you are not happy and not working on yourself, you will attract those types of people.

Don't blame others

Things are not always going to go right. If you think that things are, you're lying to yourself. We can hope and pray for the best, but at the end of the day, whatever happens, you need to deal with it and accept it. If you fall, figure out why and try again.

The way I approach things is, what's the problem, how can I solve it, and keep moving. You have to have a plan, and as things go on, you have to reorganize the plan until you have accomplished it. The bottom line is never give up and keep trying. Something has to give. If you try long enough, you will figure it out, or someone will see you trying and come along to help. But don't blame others for your mistakes. Learn from them and figure out why it didn't work, and stick to it. Understand it's not going to be easy, but if you stick with it long enough, you will figure it out. That's why it's ok to cry. It happens; sometimes you need to let it out. Maybe you don't need to cry, but you need to get it off your chest. Find someone that you trust who will be there to listen. Sometimes you need just that.

For many years, I just wanted to sing on a tour. I tried

everything I knew. I talked to everyone I could, and I constantly called and emailed people who were singing overseas and living my dream. Many times I was offered jobs, but something always happened, and it would fall through. This cycle went on for 12 years. I got a chance to go to Japan, and I did four 3-month tours. I then decided to go back to the states to try the music industry in Los Angeles, and then Las Vegas. I needed to get it out of my system, and I wanted the experience. Then I realized for me, I had a better chance overseas to do what I wanted. Sing constantly and live comfortably. So I decided it was time to focus on going overseas again. This time it took another 10 years. But I never gave up!!! I knew that I wanted to live this kind of life since the 90's. And I was never going to give up. Thank goodness, because it paid off in the long run. So I was waiting and waiting for someone to send me, and that was taking forever. I did a cruise ship in 2012 for 3 months and loved the lifestyle and the experience, so I decided I would go live abroad. I made my plan and decided that if I had no offers, I would leave in July 2013 to join a band in Vietnam. I saved my money and had a backup plan to teach English in case things didn't work out. Well, good thing I had a backup plan because once I arrived and found out there was no band, no gigs, and we were starting a new band, which quickly disbanded, I thankfully had a plan. I would give the situation 30 days. When not practicing with the band, I would go around applying for teaching jobs and try to get noticed by hitting any open stages to let people know I was in town. By the time the band ended, I was working a teaching job and 2 night clubs and and networking in my spare time. Eventually, I answered an ad and got hired to go to Dubai. But that took living in Vietnam for 9 months before I was noticed. So you have to have savings, patience, and prayer to wait out the time.

Looking in the mirror

What worked for me was to look at myself in the mirror. Be honest with yourself and make a clear inventory of your skills. Before I left the country, I had this talk with myself. I knew I was not especially pretty, but I'm cute. I was not small, but I had a voice that most said they could feel so much emotion when I sang. I knew and believed I had something. I know I'm not the best singer, but I can hold my own on any stage. Then I looked at the fact that I was good with children and had over 7 years of teaching experience. That means something, especially living abroad. I was also a great networker and easy to get along with. That was enough for me to believe in myself and take a chance. I was so tired of waiting for others to get me overseas or looking for musicians who wanted to travel. This way, I could go alone and join a band. But I had prepared myself that if things didn't go right, I would keep pushing alone.

While I did, I didn't want to, but once I realized that the situation wasn't right for me, I just moved to plan B. I got out there, and I got noticed. Sometimes you may have to do it on your own. The sooner you accept that, the better. Don't get me wrong, if you have a partner or friend who wants to join forces, that's great.

But you need to know you may have to do it alone. Be prepared!!!! Face your fears and just try. If you fail, well, at least you tried.

Waking up on top

So we are clear, I'm not rich. But I'm comfortable and living my dreams daily. I now know that I can do anything and I don't need anyone. Funny thing is, now I always get offers to join bands and groups. I believe that they see that determination in me, that they know if I'm involved, I will help to see it through. But I'm at that age where I'm done doing anything other than working on me. I'm not saying I won't join something in the future, but I will always have my own thing going on. I don't like depending on others and drama. That's why now I'm actually working on being a solo act. Singing and playing, I have a long way to go, but I know if I keep at it, I will shine. Also, so we are clear, just because I'm where I want to be now, doesn't mean I'm done working. Oh no, the work has just begun. I'm so excited to see where I will be in 5, 10, and 15 years. I'm sure I will be even happier.

Notes

Always remember to laugh

This is my favorite thing to do. Sometimes things are so crazy, you just have to laugh out loud or cry. After laughing, it's just amazing the feeling you get. I try to laugh at least a couple of times a day. I usually watch one of my favorite shows or movies. Whatever it takes to get myself out of a funk or just to keep me going. I love to laugh; sometimes I'm laughing so hard I'll actually start crying. That's the best!!! Remember to laugh on this journey; life is too short to be angry. If you are not happy, then get happy. Figure out what makes you happy and go for it. It's never too late to try something new. It is so important to be at peace with what you are doing and where you are in your life. You make the rules, and you have the power. Just do the work and make it happen. Also, if you feel that someone has done you wrong, you may have to be the bigger person and forgive that person so you can move on to where you need to be.

Whatever it takes to get you started on your journey, do it. You will never regret moving on to your purpose.

Rules to live by

Make a plan, work at it, ask questions, and try to keep at it. Never give up on your dream, and never let anyone tell you it can't be done. Stay motivated by talking to people living their dreams. Watch videos about famous/local artists and listen to their stories. As you are moving along your journey, if something is not working, then try something else. Just keep trying, remember nobody is perfect. But if you stick with it long enough, you will get better, and you will have a story to tell.

Now think about all that we talked about, and I want you to answer these 10 questions and reflect. This will help you to start towards building a solid foundation.

What does a "better life" look like to me in my most authentic vision?

Reflection

Reflection

What beliefs or habits currently hold me back from achieving this vision?

____

____

____

____

____

____

____

____

____

____

____

____

____

____

____

____

Reflection

Reflection

Reflection

How do I feel about my current relationships, and which ones support my growth versus drain it?

Reflection

Reflection

Reflection

What small, daily action can I take this week to align with my goals?

Reflection

Reflection

Reflection

When was the last time I felt truly proud of myself, and what was happening then?

Reflection

Reflection

Reflection

What fears do I have about stepping out of my comfort zone, and how can I reframe them?

____

____

____

____

____

____

____

____

____

____

____

____

____

____

____

Reflection

Reflection

Reflection

What does self-care look like for me, and how can I make it a non-negotiable practice?

Reflection

Reflection

Reflection

Who inspires me, and what qualities do they have that I can embody in my own life?

____

____

____

____

____

____

____

____

____

____

____

____

____

____

____

Reflection

Reflection

Reflection

In what areas do I need more clarity or learning, and how can I start acquiring that knowledge?

____

____

____

____

____

____

____

____

____

____

____

____

____

____

____

____

Reflection

Reflection

Reflection

What am I most grateful for today, and how can I use that gratitude to fuel my next step?

Reflection

Reflection

Reflection

Dedication

To all my friends and family who have supported me through thick and thin.

A special shout-out to my mama, who has shown me the way. My daddy, who is not with us, has made an everlasting impression on me and made me who I am today.

About the Author

Melanie was born and raised in Toledo, Ohio. She has worked in Sales, Education & Entertainment. She has traveled to over 50 countries and has a great, optimistic view of life. Anything is possible if you work hard and go for it. Her motto is "Let's make it happen". She brings you life experience and hope for the future.

www.ingramcontent.com/pod-product-compliance
Lightning Source LLC
Chambersburg PA
CBHW050803160726
48004CB00002B/684